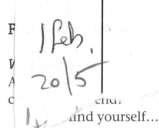

... find yourself...

- grieving, or feeling angry or scared?
- swamped by all the paperwork involved?
- wondering how best to look after yourself and your family?

Separation and divorce can feel overwhelming, but they do not have to defeat you.
  This book explains:

- what you need to do and when;
- how to cope when all you want to do is curl up in bed;
- how to move into a new life and learn to enjoy it.

This book comes with you on every step of a journey you had no intention of taking.

I was lucky enough to have four friends who had survived or were coping with divorce, or the end of a long-term relationship, about the same time as I was. Their advice, lessons, laughter, love, and support are in this book, so I dedicate it to them:

Sarah, Peta, Jenny, and Karen...
dear friends, and survivors of: numpty-ness!; just one more drink!; divorce (T.E.) alley!; and hold your balls!

And to my friends Liz, Thea, and Bridget, my goddaughter, and my own daughters, in the hope they never need *to read this book.*

First Steps through Separation and Divorce

Penny Rich

LION

Copyright © 2012 Penny Rich
This edition copyright © 2012 Lion Hudson

The author asserts the moral right
to be identified as the author of this work

A Lion Book
an imprint of
Lion Hudson plc
Wilkinson House, Jordan Hill Road,
Oxford OX2 8DR, England
www.lionhudson.com
ISBN 978 0 7459 5536 0

Distributed by:
UK: Marston Book Services, PO Box 269,
Abingdon, Oxon, OX14 4YN
USA: Trafalgar Square Publishing, 814
N. Franklin Street, Chicago, IL 60610
USA Christian Market: Kregel Publications,
PO Box 2607, Grand Rapids, MI 49501

First edition 2012
10 9 8 7 6 5 4 3 2 1 0

A catalogue record for this book is available
from the British Library

Typeset in 10/13 ITC Stone Serif
Printed and bound in Malta

Contents

Introduction

What is this book about?

divorce / di-vors / **[noun]**: the legal dissolution of a
marriage by decree; [singular] a separation between
things which were or ought to be connected.
ORIGIN French, from Latin *divortium*;
DERIVATIVE **divorcement, divorcee**

That is the *Oxford English Dictionary* (Oxford University
Press) definition, and this, from the voice of experience,
is mine:

*To survive, a healthy, long-term marriage of heart and
mind relies on mutual respect, trust, love, kindness, caring,
commitment, teamwork, and, above all, the ability to grow
and change together – without these things, it will die.*

My definition is human, but it is also quite a lot to ask of
two human beings in the twenty-first century, when we
strive to have rights, be independent, and be individual
in all things. So it is little wonder that the two countries
in the Western world that offer the most freedom – the

UK and the US – both currently have nearly half of *all* marriages ending in divorce. In the UK an average marriage lasts eleven and a half years, but if you just "live together" (cohabit), the average relationship lasts only three years (Office of National Statistics).

So, if you are facing the end of your marriage or relationship, you are not alone. There are hundreds of thousands of others going through exactly the same thing, right now. Separation or divorce is listed in the top five most stressful life experiences – along with bereavement, moving house, getting married, or changing your job. Yet the end of a relationship involves aspects of all *five* of these things – loss; packing, downsizing, and moving; deciding and planning many things in a short time; living within a reduced income or finding ways to increase it – plus blame, fear, grief, fury, chaos, and emotional turmoil. That's what this book is about: the journey through the end of a relationship and how you can find ways to cope with it.

Who is this book for?

I hope this book helps everybody, on all sides of what is the ending of the happy-ever-after story. The truth is that we can no longer bear to be with the person we once loved enough to choose in the first place, which is why breaking up is so devastating, difficult, and painful. So this book is for everyone who is affected:

- Men or women, mothers or fathers, family or friends, married couples, or unmarried partners.
- Everyone who has a relationship that has hit a bad patch – whether you stay together, separate, or divorce.

- Any friends, family, or children who are sharing the end of the story.
- Everyone making this hazardous journey – step by step – through separation and divorce.

How should you use this book?

However you wish – if you need one chapter first, go straight to it. But I have tried to write it in the order that events usually unfold, to assist every step of the way. You might read some chapters before your own journey has reached that stage, but forearmed is forewarned, and it might open your eyes, heart, and mind to what lies ahead.

Very loosely, the chapters cover the following:

- the **decision**
- the emotional **repercussions**
- the legal **practicalities**
- **healing** some of the pain
- coping with **change** and chaos
- dealing with **worry** and fear
- trying to be **positive**
- trying to let go of anger and **revenge**
- how to **communicate** with your ex
- how to embrace and **rejoice** in a new life.

Why did I write this book?

I was one of five friends (with fourteen children between us!) facing separation or divorce about the same time, and although our journeys were different, we all seemed to go through similar stages at similar times. So what you will find in this book is very personal and practical advice, gathered from some very sensible sources. There might be some humorous chapter headings (laughing helped us through *our* journeys), but there are serious lessons on every page.

This book is not about me; it is about *you* and your journey into what seems like a dead end (divorce alley) but actually leads to a new beginning (the daredevil divorcee). My story pops up now and then, where applicable, but so you understand it, here is the outline: after twenty-two years of marriage my divorce was finalized after a long and acrimonious year, in 2009; there were no third parties involved; my ex-husband does not communicate with me now; my teenage daughters chose not to see or speak to me for over a year; and I am still not "over it", as they say. But time is a great healer and I no longer wake with a lump like a brick in my heart. I really try to enjoy my new life.

Divorce is an odyssey, and, like all great adventures, you learn much about yourself and life along the way. I hope reading this book helps make *your* journey easier.

If you want to discuss anything about this book, share your story, or see what happens next, please visit my website: **www.pennyrichthewriter.com**.

1

Breaking up
(... is hard to do)

If you are reading this book, you have already lived
through some part of your relationship breaking down.
Separation and divorce don't just happen, like coming
down with measles, and you don't just stop loving
someone overnight. For some time – weeks, months,
possibly years – you might have been to-ing and fro-ing
on whether to make the **decision** (and that's what this
chapter is about) to end your relationship. And this means
your recent life has had unhappiness, rows, burying your
head in the sand, disagreements, emotional turmoil, and
the worst dilemma of adult life: do I fight to save my
marriage, do I keep trying to repair the relationship, or do
I quit?

There is no easy answer, especially if children are
involved or you have been in the relationship for some
time. The ultimate decision depends very much on

the reasons why *you* feel your love is over. It could be that you have just grown apart and have been leading separate lives for some time anyway. It could be your partner has walked out and left you with no choice in the matter. Your relationship might have involved mental or physical cruelty. Perhaps you have lived with a liar and no longer trust them, or you have financial difficulties or other personal issues that have come between you. Maybe they were unfaithful, maybe you bickered all the time, or there was a lack of mutual respect, a lack of sex, a lack of care and feeling loved. Maybe you just felt trapped or suffocated.

There are many reasons to choose from, but the root of *all* failed relationships is that if you can't grow and change together, you eventually have differing needs and outgrow one another. Once you were like two peas in a pod, but things change (even pods!), and with time life is more complicated, so that even the things you loved about each other (*s/he's so laid back and funny*) become things you dislike (*why does s/he leave the toothpaste lid off, then tell me to chill?*).

No matter what your personal reasons are, all break-ups have one thing in common: it takes much time and heartache to decide to end it with someone you once loved enough to marry or to commit to "for ever".

Mythbuster

Separating or getting divorced is the easy way out.
No, it isn't. Leaving a relationship is one of the hardest challenges you will face in life.

Are you sure?

Although finally facing the fact that your relationship is over comes as a shock, it also comes as a relief. There is so much pain and unhappiness in life, but most of us eventually reach a point where we can't take any more – which invariably means life-changing decisions are made when we've reached crisis point! So it is very important to be clear about why *you* have reached the end of this relationship, because that will give you the strength to get through what lies ahead and to embrace a new and different future.

When you are feeling hurt, rejected, and angry (and at this point during the end of my marriage, I certainly did), it is very easy just to jump on the divorce bandwagon and go full steam ahead. Or, if you are sure of your choices and understand your reasons, you might just be pleased it is over and you are about to start again. Either way, before you do anything else, step back from the misery and emotion, and ask the following three questions:

- Have I given this relationship my best shot?

- If I end this relationship, will I be unhappier than I am now?

- Is there anything I feel I want to do to save this relationship?

Answer as honestly as possible, write down all your thoughts, and then see how you feel about your answers. But exclude any external influences. For instance, both finances and children ought to be left out because:

- a happy parent makes a happy child;
- children grow up and leave home, but you still have *your* life to live, happily;
- money can't buy happiness or love.

It is important to understand your decision, and at the end of the day this decision is about *you*, and *your* partner, and *your* relationship. Knowing and understanding why you feel it is over will help you cope with the feelings of loss, failure, and fear that inevitably follow the breakdown of a long (and once loving) relationship.

If your answers have made you think again or if you still have some doubts, remember...

 ✔ It's OK...

... to change your mind.
Most people work hard to save their failing marriage and don't give up on a whim.

If you are not *quite* sure

The one thing that makes a major choice or decision clearer is talking about it. Talking to someone you trust, and listening to what they say, helps you make up your own mind – and when your heart is hurting, it is quite hard to ignore it and use your head. So, if there is still any doubt, seek out some very good friends, and share your concerns or dilemmas with them. But, in the heat of the moment (be warned!), it is important not to "dish" or disclose anything about your partner you might regret, or that might embarrass you if you have second thoughts and eventually decide the relationship isn't 100 per cent over.

Remember: you can change your mind even if you have told an awful lot of people an awful lot of reasons why you are glad to be rid of your partner.

If you prefer advice from a less personal source, approach a professional – someone from your church, or a trained mediator, marriage guidance expert, or counsellor (see the **Useful resources** section at the back of the book) and discuss your concerns with them, because those concerns will remain confidential.

No matter whether you choose friends or professionals for support, don't necessarily follow their advice to the letter (particularly if they say what you *should* do; it's about *could* – there is no right or wrong), but use them as a sounding board to help decide what is right for you. Once you have done this, either way your decision will be the right one.

Two little words: It's over.

Now, to deal briefly with conscience. Some of us take our vows very seriously (*till death us do part*), and if you do, you need to ask yourself how relevant that is if a marriage is already dead. As for those feelings of guilt or failure or misgivings (*should I, would I, could I?*), you need to remember that you have made the right choice for the right reasons. All the "ifs" and "buts" need to be laid to rest. But, before we move on to face the repercussions of this choice, there is a **self-help** task on the following page, designed to ease your way into all that lies ahead.

As an exercise in helping yourself in a difficult time, this is very cathartic. It will reassure you that you made a decision at the right time for the right reasons, and, more importantly, that you *chose* to do so. It is also reassuring to understand that you might not always feel the way you do at the moment, and however good or bad a situation is, it will change.

Self-help

Coming to terms with your decision

This exercise is a chance to write down a list of all the reasons why you think this relationship is over – and since no one else will read it (you're going to rip it up afterwards!), you can be as honest, sad, mad, and ruthless as you feel.

Grab a sheet of paper and a pen, and draw up three columns, titled as below:

My reasons for why our relationship is over...	How I feel about these reasons now...	How I might feel about them in the future...

Take a deep breath (it calms the mind) and write down anything and everything you want to – from the silliest little things to the darkest, meanest thoughts. Afterwards, look carefully at what you have written, and again a few days later, and then either put the piece of paper away in a safe place, or burn it (a symbolic way to lay thoughts to rest!). I hope it gives you some comfort to know that you made a positive choice here. The reality from now on is that if you can make peace with the present, it won't impact so much on your future.

2

Breaking out
(... or breaking down)

You have made the decision that it's over and you probably feel relief, a sense of breaking free, that there is an escape from misery. Beyond that, there are always **repercussions** to decisions. So how long you were together as a couple and how you feel about the relationship ending determine what happens next. Once the initial euphoria subsides, what usually follows is a tidal wave of emotion. And since crying releases pent-up emotions, expect to break down and cry your heart out, or at the very least feel tearful at the most unexpected moments.

They are unexpected because the sadness will creep up on you and catch you unawares – it could be while you are making the family's favourite dinner, or opening a letter addressed to "Mr and Mrs", or after sympathy and a kind word from someone. One of my most unexpected sob-till-you-snort scenes was in the reception area of a health centre. As I was paying a bill, the computer threw up my birth date, and the staff mischievously sang "Happy Birthday" to me. So, alone on my fiftieth birthday, I repaid the kindness of two complete strangers by howling like a banshee! And I couldn't stop until I had got through half a box of tissues and ruined any possible benefit to those innocent people having aromatherapy treatments behind closed doors. To this day, I tell myself that this was perfectly normal behaviour – and that's what you must do, too.

Feeling sad, bereft, and devastated at the loss of an important relationship is utterly normal. Whether you leave, or have been left, there is still a loss. And the misery that then engulfs you might be unwanted, but it is *necessary* to help you come to terms with the immense loss of what *was* and what *might have been* in your life – all those memories, hopes, plans, and dreams are now, instantly, a thing of the past.

> ✔ It's OK...

... to cry.
It's much healthier and less stressful to let emotion out, rather than to bottle it up.

The good grief
Experts liken the emotional impact of a separation or divorce to that of a death in the immediate family, and there are five widely accepted stages of coming to terms with loss. But how long the process takes and how easy it is for you personally is impossible to second-guess. Most people take from eighteen months to four years to feel

whole and happy again after a relationship ends. Some get over it in six months; others are still struggling decades later. There is no right or wrong, and anyone who says "It's time to move on, you need to get over it" deserves a quick kick in the shins.

You will also find you dip in and out of these five emotional stages. They are like sharks, circling randomly, and just when you think you are safe on the other side of anger or depression, it will lurch up and consume you all over again. The emotional journey is up to you, but at some point you will probably pass through some if not all of these five stages. To help you recognize them, see if anything below sounds familiar:

- *Shock/denial* – You might catch yourself saying: "It's just a midlife crisis, he will come back"; "Surely this isn't happening to us?"; "I thought we were happy, and now this"; "We haven't had any *us* time for ages, but we can work it out."

- *Anger/resentment* – You might catch yourself saying: "How dare she treat me like this – she never loved me anyway"; "I'll never forgive him for what he's done"; "What a two-timing, lying, cheating, bullying, immature, selfish imbecile I married"; "I hope she rots in hell, I want to..."

- *Bargaining/pleading* – You might catch yourself saying: "Please God, if you make him come back, I promise I'll..."; "I've changed, honey; let me prove to you why you want me back"; "I know you still love me. I'll do anything you want; just tell me what."

- *Guilt/depression* –You might catch yourself saying: "I can't cope with any more of this"; "Will the pain ever end?"; "My life is over. I am ugly, fat, worthless, and no one will ever love me"; "All of this is my fault. If only I..."; "I don't know what to do..."; "Nobody cares."

- *Acceptance/hope* – You might catch yourself saying: "I don't like this, but I will get through it"; "I can't keep wallowing in the past"; "OK, there's nothing more I can do"; "It's over, and I've got to carry on and keep going."

The bad feelings

So now you know what you might say as you go through the journey of impending separation or divorce, but what might you *feel*? At the start of this chapter, I described it as a tidal wave of emotions because that's what it felt like to me – a churning, swirling torrent that submerges your every waking moment and seeps into your turbulent dreams. Those experts who describe it as "the five stages of grief" make it sound easy, but it's not. Some days you might feel any or all of the following:

shock, turmoil, worry, grief, anxiety, sadness, abandoned, scared, guilty, ashamed, unappreciated, unwanted, unloved, unattractive, upset, lacking in energy, in a low mood, panic, anger, indecisive, tearful, fearful, furious, heartbroken, lost, forlorn, a failure, stressed out, unable to sleep, hostile, distraught, regretful, lonely.

Over the next few weeks, you might like to tick any of those words you feel – you might be quite surprised at how many emotions are raging away (two years ago, I would have ticked all of them in a mere twenty-four hours, plus a few others besides!). Try to keep reminding yourself this is normal, it's healthy, it's part of the journey, and don't beat yourself up thinking you are ridiculous or a basket case, or that you've got to get a grip. You will get a grip on reality again, you will stop shedding tears, and you will love yourself and life – and even laugh again. It just takes time.

However, as you go through the stages, if the grief turns to depression, if you really can't cope with everything life is hurling at you, then you might need to get some medical support and speak to your doctor. The signs to watch out for are:

• being unable to sleep or get out of bed;

• feeling life isn't worth living and contemplating ending it;

• not bothering to take a shower, dress, put on make-up;

• not wanting to go out;

• crying at some point every day and night after six months;

• being unable to enjoy food, exercise, reading, outings – or anything you once enjoyed;

• feeling tired, exhausted, unable to relax, unable to make decisions, or that everything is pointless.

These symptoms mean you may need professional help (see the **Useful resources** section at the back of the book). During my divorce – which on a scale of 1 to 10, from good to bad, rates about 9.8 – one of my daughters was put on antidepressants, much to my fear, guilt, and shame. However, it was temporary, and helped at a time when she needed help. It is important, in times of need, to forget about "being strong" and "being weak" and do what helps *you* cope. So, if you know you are not dealing with your grief, put your hand up and seek professional help.

Mythbuster

Giving up on my relationship means I've failed.
No, it doesn't. It takes two people to make a marriage work.

The ugly thoughts
The tidal wave of emotion has an underlying swirl of flotsam and jetsam – basically, an eddy of bad thoughts about you, your life, your dilemma, your flaws, your future. This can make you feel hideous, useless, horrid, ugly, and unhappy – and that's on a good day! Again, you have to go with the flow (it will get better), but to put this negativity back in perspective you need to make time every day for positive reinforcement.

 Remember: never feel sorry for yourself – or at least don't do it for too long!

It is important to find some tiny piece of calm within the emotional storm. However you do it depends on what you personally find helpful, but try to resist drinking too much alcohol or smoking like a chimney – with time they will make you feel worse, not better.

The one thing that helped me was to set aside five minutes every morning and every night to restore my inner spirit. For me, it involved a self-deprecating laugh and some peace. You might choose to have a quiet, contemplative moment, or to pray, meditate, do some stretches, have a cup of tea, watch the sun rise and set, or even to think about how much you have achieved. Whatever you do, it will help. But if you really want to destroy ugly thoughts, try to find something that helps you rediscover your sense of humour. Laughter, even if you are laughing darkly, is a great cure in adversity.

Self-help

Coming to terms with turmoil

This exercise is a suggestion (it worked for me) – feel free to substitute or adapt to suit your needs, but do *something* every morning and evening, no matter what.

Every morning, when you wake up, say something positive. Try a "mantra" or "positive thought" that you repeat every day for a week and that means something to you personally. Here are some examples of mine (and of the many friends and some relatives who joined in the game and emailed me suggestions as the weeks went by):

Some of my (printable) wake-up weekly mantras:

- All is not lost.

- This soon shall pass.

- Life can be cruel.

- The sun will shine (again).

- I married him, so I've only myself to blame.

- Whatever I've done, I'm sorry.

- Be brave, little Noddy, all will be well.

- Give a man an inch and he thinks he's a ruler.

- I have an angel on my shoulder.

- Spawn of the devil!
- God, let me live long enough to see him buried.

Every evening, if possible just before bed, sit comfortably, breathe deeply and slowly, and try to find inner peace, a calm place inside you, and let go of any worries, anxieties, and stress. I am not very good at stopping troubled thoughts, so I'd start with any *positives* before trying to find calm.

Five things I have achieved today:

- I cleaned my teeth.
- I got to the bottom of our bank overdraft.
- I cooked a delicious chicken risotto.
- I spoke (and listened to) three good friends.
- I didn't cry when I opened my lawyer's bill.

The calm in the storm
Think of somewhere or something special or sacred to you, then imagine you are there and push other thoughts aside – perhaps lying on a beach, reciting a favourite poem, prayer, or song, a childhood memory... Think of nothing but that "place" and stay in it as long as possible, breathing deeply all the while.

3

The legal stuff
(... a necessary evil)

We all know how marriages start, but most of us have little experience of how they end – possibly apart from people such as Zsa Zsa Gabor (eight divorces), or Lana Turner, Mickey Rooney, Liz Taylor, and Larry King (seven divorces each)! So this chapter needs to start with the **practicalities** and legalities of ending a marriage, before we move on to personal choices and decisions. Think of the next few pages as a quick and very simple guide on English divorce law to bring you up to speed. If you live in any other country, find relevant information from local websites that explains all of this in greater detail (see the **Useful resources** section at the back of the book).

Note: If you are one of the four million couples in the UK who have been cohabiting in a long-term relationship (that is, living together but *not* married), you need to understand that this does not give you the same legal rights as for couples in a legal marriage or civil partnership (which, in the UK, ends with a civil partnership dissolution).

Unless a "common law" husband and wife drafted a "living together agreement" which is legally binding, the end of the relationship is only regulated by property law and not by family law in the UK – so, for instance, an unmarried father has no automatic legal rights or responsibilities to his children or partner. However, in some parts of Australia, Canada, America, and Scandinavia, common law couples do have the same legal rights as married ones.

If you are unmarried, you may skip what follows and turn to page 31 (*Reality versus legality*) – or, to find out how to better understand your legal rights at this point, turn to the **Useful resources** section at the back of the book.

A quick guide to legal speak

Be warned: this stage of your journey brings a new challenge – understanding the gobbledegook (otherwise known as legal terminology) that is thrust upon you. Here is a quick translation of the most common phrases you may encounter:

- The *petitioner* is the name for whichever one of you "legally" instigates divorce.

- The *respondent* is the name for the one who is on the receiving end of the divorce.

- The *grounds for divorce* are the reasons you believe the marriage is over (see below).

- The *divorce petition* is an application for divorce put before the court and served on your partner. It ends, poignantly, with *the prayer* that the marriage be dissolved.

- The *acknowledgement of service* is the document your partner returns to the court to agree to divorce.
- The *statement of arrangements for children* is what you have agreed on residence, contact, care, and maintenance for children under sixteen, or eighteen if still in education.
- The *decree nisi* is the piece of paper saying that your divorce is agreed.
- The *decree absolute* is the piece of paper saying that your divorce is now legal.
- *Maintenance* is money paid – either monthly or as a lump sum – to support your partner financially.
- *Child maintenance* is money paid monthly towards the child's financial needs.
- A *clean break* is a lump sum (paid in lieu of maintenance) taken from the joint assets (before they are divided) and given as full and final settlement to one partner.

If you agree on sharing marital assets and children, and if it goes according to plan, there should be no more terminology thrown at you. If not, be prepared to seek legal help as it will save you endless headaches (for example, *affidavits*, *consent orders*, *Form A* for ancillary relief, *Form E* for assessing and valuing assets, *maintenance orders*).

A quick guide to the grounds for divorce

One of my happily married girlfriends jokes that in every marriage more than a week old there are grounds for divorce; however, to get divorced in the UK you must have been married for more than one year. The only legally accepted grounds for divorces are that the marriage has "irretrievably broken down".

There are five ways of showing this:

- That the respondent has committed adultery (and your spouse must consent to this).
- That the respondent has behaved in such a way that there are grounds for unreasonable behaviour.
- That the respondent has deserted you for the previous two years (rarely used these days).
- That you have been separated for the past two years (the respondent must consent).
- That you have been separated for the past five years (you do not need the respondent's consent).

Most people opt for "unreasonable behaviour" and you then need to list your *actual* grounds for divorce (for instance, five to ten examples of "unreasonable behaviour" throughout the marriage), but no matter what you say, it must be turned into the puzzling language of legal speak. For example:

- "My ex drinks like a fish and becomes abusive" is translated to "The respondent regularly consumes alcohol, which has a detrimental effect on his/her behaviour and moods".
- "My ex badmouths and belittles and bullies me" is translated to "The respondent denigrates the petitioner's abilities in front of family, friends, and colleagues".

✔ It's OK...

... to say what *you* want.
During divorce you both have equal rights and needs.

A quick guide to the great divide

Generally speaking, if a marriage ends in the UK, the following applies (although there are exceptions – length of marriage, number and age of children, inheritance, financial contribution, need – and, take note, it can go either way when parents disagree and the court decides for you). The usual is:

- An equal division of marital assets, after debts, on a 50/50 shared basis.

- Shared access to children (usually every other weekend, half the holidays, and sometimes one evening per week) for the parent with whom they don't live.

- The legal requirement for a father to provide maintenance for children: he should pay a *minimum* of 15 per cent (one child) and up to 25 per cent (three or more children) of his net annual income.

- The requirement for some lifelong (or until the age of retirement or the point at which any children reach the age of eighteen) maintenance for a wife, particularly if she has been a "housewife", the husband has earning potential, historically he has been the breadwinner, and the funds are available.

- Pension sharing: any existing private pension funds or schemes are divided equally.

Reality versus legality

Now we have looked at legalities, it's time to look at realities, because what this entire chapter really depends on is how amicably and maturely you and your soon-to-be-ex are dealing with the end of your relationship. There are some couples who manage to be friendly and adult in crisis, and who put the needs of all family members above their own.

 Remember: avoid disparaging someone to a third party – it's usually you who will sound bad!

If you are one of them, you are very lucky, and you and your partner might manage a happy, healthy, positive (and relatively inexpensive) separation or divorce. And this is the best way by far – for you, your partner, your family, and your friends. If you both agree the finances and any decisions on children or housing, you may choose at this point just to separate, which you can do without actually getting divorced – but you will need a *separation agreement* (either drawn up by a lawyer or you can buy one online). This will legally formalize what you have agreed, and a separation period often gives couples time to consider the decision and undergo marriage counselling if both parties want to. Or, if you choose to divorce, you can buy legal do-it-yourself divorce kits online, which will save money on lawyers.

However, statistics show that most people start out intending to be amicable and end up with something nearer Armageddon. If, like me, you are one of the unlucky ones, rest assured you are not alone. This is because, at this point in the break-up game, self-interest rears its ugly head, particularly when it comes to sharing the assets and even the children, the furniture, any debts, any pets...

From my personal experience, divorce began with my husband saying, "I will always look after you, nothing will change", and – three months later, when I chose not to agree with what he wanted – turned into "How dare you steal half my money?" To my shame, this caused us both a year of stress and discord, during which we spent tens of thousands of pounds on lawyers and court cases (in fact, I spent 4 per cent of my half share of the joint marital assets I eventually received). I never thought this could possibly happen, but it did, because at the time there seemed no other way – we couldn't come to a decision, and we needed a judge to do it for us. So, at this point, you need to ask yourself the following questions:

- Do I believe my partner will do all the things we have agreed, without reneging?

- Do I think that what I expect/want is as fair and valid as what my partner says they expect/want?

If you answer "Yes" to both questions, you may be able to end your relationship with a do-it-yourself divorce (see the **Useful resources** section at the back of the book) – the cheapest option at about £3,000. If you answer "Yes" to one question and "No" to the other, you may be able to get divorced with the help of a mediation lawyer – this will resolve your differences without going to court (about £3,000–6,000). If you answer "No" to both questions, you should consider finding a good lawyer to assist you with the process (if you end up in court several times, it's about £10,000–30,000; or up to about £50,000, if neither partner relents).

Mythbuster

Lawyers are only out to make money from your divorce.
Absolutely not. The good ones are a necessary evil: they hold your hand as they explain your rights and help you achieve them.

How to find a good lawyer

- Best advice: you need a lawyer specializing in family law (that means divorce) who also offers collaborative or mediation services (to resolve differences *without* going to court, thereby saving costs), and who is a member of the nationwide UK lawyers association called Resolution (they practise a non-confrontational approach).

- Don't be frightened to shop around. Would you buy the first car you ever saw?

- Treat it like a career decision – *network*. Ask any divorcees you know (particularly any divorced lawyers who divorced a lawyer!), any lawyers you know, friends, or even a total stranger who isn't wearing a wedding ring...

- Look on the internet for recommended family lawyers in your area (but I would advise you to avoid any that advertise "No win, no fees" because presumably you want to win?), and look in the phone book because you want a local lawyer.

- And, most importantly, follow every word in the **self-help** guide below.

Coming to terms with a lawyer

This exercise is all about practicalities. It is equally about self-pain and self-gain, because sometimes in life effort reaps rewards. You need to pick three lawyers, set up initial one-hour consultations (these are usually free, or cost £50–70 an hour – check costs when you first phone), and be prepared to make every minute count. First, do your homework – this is my best advice, from my personal experience:

- Take with you a list of everything you want to ask/need to know as an agenda on a single sheet of A4 paper.

- Put this same agenda to all three lawyers. At the end of the one-hour consultation, leave saying only that you will come back to them by a certain date.

- Compare their answers, and pick the one who best provides the most helpful response to your questions and the best solutions to your needs – but please take into account your feelings also. For me, my instinct favoured one particular female lawyer – and this turned out to be a blessing, as she was professional, sensible, and caring (when I twice burst into hysterical tears on the phone, she calmly advised me, but kindly didn't charge me).

Note: When you instruct a lawyer to act on your behalf, you need to provide proof of identity (for example, a passport), a copy of your marriage certificate, and (often) a deposit to be deducted from your final settlement and bill.

Draw up the agenda on a single sheet of A4 paper.

Part one (fifteen minutes of the discussion)

- *The marriage and reasons for the divorce*
  Try to keep this to one paragraph. You need to explain when you were married; number and ages of any children; why you feel the marriage is over.

- *The current financial situation*
  List (keep this to two paragraphs) your partner's income and yours; any known debts; regular outgoings (school fees, a mortgage, rent, hire purchases, joint bank accounts or credit cards) and future assets (for example, inheritance, pensions); current lifestyle (holidays, cars, educational needs, paid help, dental and medical outgoings, and so on). You don't have to have exact figures.

Part two (twenty minutes of the discussion)

- *The current points of disagreement between you and your spouse*
  Try to keep it brief and polite.

- *What you would hope to get emotionally and financially from the divorce settlement*
  For example: I would like to keep the marital home; I would like to sell the marital home; I would like to keep looking after the children and not return to work until they are in tertiary education; I would like my partner to help with child care; I would like to take my partner for all they've got; I would like to resolve our differences as inexpensively as possible.

Part three (twenty minutes of the discussion)

- *What would they advise/how would they suggest resolving your differences?*
  Take notes, listen to what they say, and try not to interrupt with more than a necessary question (although you can always email these later, for free, as part of your consultation!).

Part four (five minutes... or as long as they keep talking)

- *What are the costs likely to be at each stage of the divorce?*
- *How often do they bill and what charges are specifically itemized on the bill?*
- *How would they proceed if you did not have the funds to pay until after a divorce settlement was reached?*
- *Is there anything else they want to tell you at this point?*

Note: If they don't offer, ask for a copy of their terms and conditions (to read later); if they don't have such a thing, they are unprofessional and immediately bottom of the list.

4

The broken heart (... how can you mend it?)

This chapter is about **healing** the hurt (or starting to try to), but first it is time to take stock. You have decided it is over, and even if you are glad it's over, you are caught up in a torrent of emotions, have had to confront the legal processes of break-up, and have probably thought way too much about all the changes and choices coming your way. Oh, and don't forget that you have to keep on top of the job – whether that's being a good parent, a professional employee or employer, or all three! Yes, and those two little words "It's over" have spread like wildfire, so you have to talk about this – to friends, family, your children, your partner – without crying hysterically or acting in any way that shows this is all overwhelming.

And with reality comes the first tinge of fear: those horrid little thoughts, picking away inside your head (usually when you should be asleep) – "I'll be lonely and old, and I'll die living with five cats and no one will notice"; "I haven't sorted the valuations or copied the bank statements and bills, and they're due in tomorrow"; "What if it doesn't work out and I've made a terrible mistake?"; "How am I going to cope with so little money? There isn't even enough in the joint account to pay the mortgage this month."

Finally, let's not forget that in the middle of this turmoil, you are meant to be a dignified, sane, calm adult and instruct your lawyer! It is little wonder most couples don't have a "good" separation or divorce, because at this point everything is too much. With so much stress coming from every direction, it is hard to be reasonable and act like a grown-up, especially when you need someone to kiss it all better and make it go away.

Stress can make the most rational of people prowl the house and start sticking yellow Post-it notes on paintings and pots. In my case, stress triggered the ultimate childish spat – a fight over a ten-year-old potato masher (I eventually gift-wrapped it and gave it to my ex for Christmas!). Under pressure, we all do things we are not proud of.

Forget heartache or heartbreak...

Some days it feels as if the stress is enough to snap your heart in two. Life as you knew it has been turned upside down and you have lost your dreams for the future, your hopes and plans. In fact, your whole future as you imagined it has gone, so take time to mourn it.

 **✔ It's OK...**

... to take it one step at a time.
Try not to think beyond today. When in doubt, just take
the next small step.

So the positive thing to do at this point in the journey
through separation and divorce is to find ways to help that
broken heart, to take the pressure off, and to try to feel a
little better. We all think we will be happy ever after, but
being happier now is much more important. And since
we don't know what life is going to chuck at us tomorrow,
the future may be rosier than anyone can imagine. Sadly,
no one can wave a magic wand and make all this angst
and heartbreak disappear, but you have the power to make
some stress vanish – the "self-inflicted" kind, the "being
too hard on yourself", "glass is half empty", "thinking too
much" kind.

 **Remember: the glass is half full, never half
empty, and if you look for it, you'll find a
silver lining even in adversity.**

Here are some suggestions that might help you feel a little,
teeny, tiny bit better:

Try to give things a perspective

• Divorce is only sorting out a mistake.

• It will get better in the future.

Try to avoid the blame game and the guilt trip

- The Whys…? (*… was I so stupid? … didn't it work? … did I put up with that? … did I marry them? … did they leave?*).

- The Ifs… (*… only I had known; … I hadn't said that; … I had my time again*).

Try to look after yourself

- Constant worry and stress eventually make you ill.

- Eat, sleep, rest, relax, recharge, *and* divorce.

Try to be kind to yourself

- Self-esteem, self-confidence, and self-respect suffer during divorce.

- Give praise for how far you have come, how well you've coped, how much you have achieved.

Mythbuster

I will never find love/happiness again.
Yes, you will. But first you need to learn to love yourself!

Self-help

Coming to terms with self-love
The best way to be kind to your anguished soul, mind, heart, and emotions is to seek out some light relief, so this little self-help exercise is all about fun. If your heart really is broken (for some, it might be throbbing with joy, not pain), then it needs some tender loving care. So, as often as you humanly can, take a break from real life and laugh whenever possible. I can only suggest things I would enjoy

here. Please feel free to choose your own favourite things, particularly if you are a male reader. The bare minimum is to do *one* of the following for yourself once a week, but there is no maximum.

Desperate Divorcee Top Five Nights In	Desperate Divorcee Top Five Treats
Order a takeaway and invite round friends with shoulders (to cry on)	Do some gentle stretches and soak in a hot tub
Watch a film that makes you laugh as you cry (see Top Ten suggestions, below)	Open a box of chocolates, drink more than one glass of wine, cook your favourite meal
Lye on a sofa and talk to a friend on the phone for hours	Switch off: read a good book, a magazine, do a crossword puzzle...
Cry with laughter as you dance to a Top Ten song (see below), turned up very loud	Buy yourself something you've always wanted, or at least dream about doing it!
Learn some new talent (play the ukulele, belly dance, draw/paint or make collages with photos of your ex...)	Take a trip to the beauty parlour (a massage, facial, change your hair colour – try to resist cosmetic surgery!)

You will find your own favourite films and songs if you put your mind to it, but here are some suggestions:

Desperate Divorcee Top Ten Films	Desperate Divorcee Top Ten Songs
The First Wives Club	Yesterday (The Beatles)
Love Actually	I Will Survive (Gloria Gaynor)
The War of the Roses	Go Your Own Way (Fleetwood Mac)
Mrs Doubtfire	Que Sera Sera (Doris Day)
Mamma Mia!	Cruel Summer (Ace of Base)

The broken heart (... how can you mend it?)

Desperate Divorcee Top Ten Films	Desperate Divorcee Top Ten Songs
Shirley Valentine	50 Ways to Leave Your Lover (Paul Simon)
Groundhog Day	You're So Vain (Carly Simon)
High Fidelity	Hit the Road Jack (Ray Charles)
How Stella Got Her Groove Back	Don't Go Breakin' My Heart (Elton John, Kiki Dee)
Eternal Sunshine of the Spotless Mind	Ain't No Sunshine When She's Gone (Bill Withers)

5
The broken home
(... and all alone)

Reality check: the divorce journey has reached the stage of **change**. Major decision making is now needed – but there is no one to discuss things with (even the other half isn't there). There is no one to blame (*what if I make the wrong choice?*). And there are no simple answers any more (so many choices, so many fears, so many changes). What usually kicks in now is that you feel alone (not to mention raw and emotionally exhausted). And you are standing at the bottom of a mountain and looking up – which is the true impact of divorce: facing huge challenges.

There will be changes to what was "home", what "family" life entailed, and what you enjoyed as your "standard of living". In real life, fear releases adrenalin (you run away, or bite, fight, and attack), but in divorce it releases *indecision* – you become the bunny, caught in the headlights as you cross the road! You procrastinate! You know what you need to do, but can you do it? Probably not, so you end up doing nothing, which seems easier.

 Remember: live every day doing something that makes you smile or laugh, and avoid procrastination.

Making choices is your biggest challenge now. Do you cling in desperation to what there is (safety) or find ways to make the jump (the unknown)? It is enough to make an angel cry, let alone a mere mortal. But by now you have probably shed enough tears, so it is time to dry your eyes and try crying in a different way...

Mythbuster

Divorce brings so much unhappiness that it's better to stay in an unhappy marriage.
No! No! No! You *will* find happiness if you try to think of new beginnings (not endings), new challenges (not failures), and new chances to use your strengths (not weaknesses).

Crying wolf

I can't cope. I am all alone. I can't do this. If you remember the fable of the boy who cried wolf, you will know you have just read three examples of crying wolf when there really isn't one – what there is, is *you*, a wolf trapped in sheep's clothing. You can cope, you are not alone, and you can do this. Now is the time to take a long, hard look back at your life and think of all the hurdles you have jumped. Write them down and you'll remember your strengths.

Moving home and having to make new friends, that first day at school, finding a job, losing a job, losing a parent, having your heart broken, learning to ride a bike, retraining, restarting, starting a hobby, not getting the job, bonus, or promotion you wanted, getting sick, losing your bag on holiday, losing your savings... Some of this must have happened when you were single and had to sort it yourself.

At some point in every relationship, you lose parts of yourself (things change, you adapt, you have different priorities), and now you have to rediscover that independence and those strengths and other things you probably have not used in a long time. Rediscovering yourself is part of the journey. For me, it was that I had gone from working and being independent to having children and taking on the "Cinderella" role, while my husband managed (post-divorce, I would say mismanaged!) the finances. So, for me, post-divorce, finances seemed an insurmountable challenge until a good friend came to the rescue and taught me how to use Excel spreadsheets.

At this point you have to re-learn how to do, how to decide, and how to be the (only) adult. There are ways to deal with chaos, and you will find some of these at the end of this chapter, and many others all by yourself.

Crying help

Everyone *knows* when to ask for help. But asking for help means admitting you need it. So, as you try to rise to the challenges and get back on your feet again (and possibly move house, find a way of earning extra money, do all the things your absent partner did), you are under huge pressure to "carry on as normal", especially if you have children. At this point, the children (who are busy with their own "loss" of one parent, fear of change, confusion over loyalty, and anger that all this is happening) often behave as badly as they can!

It doesn't matter how you present it, to children divorce means uncertainty – and what children thrive on is routine. A few things help here:

- Ensure consistency and firmness (don't use children to replace your missing partner) and as much normal routine as you can muster.

- Do not *ever* let them overhear or deliberately tell them details of the divorce.

- Discourage them from taking sides.

- Never (and this is difficult) say anything negative about their absent parent.

- Encourage them to spend time with their absent parent, even if they say they don't want to. Be the best parents you can be at this stage of your life.

- Help children keep in touch with extended family, grandparents, etc.

- Be positive (not jealous!) about things they do when they are with the absent parent.

Finally – and to show why this is most important...
I know someone who watched her ex-husband shower their sons with presents (iPhones, xbox, sport shoes) every other Saturday when he took them out, while she was struggling to provide toilet rolls back at home. So one day, when her sons asked her what they were doing with Daddy on Saturday, she glibly replied, "Probably going to

Disneyland." In fact, Daddy took them round the corner for a pizza, and everyone ended up in tears. And so the last, most important, thing is...

• Do not be a competitive or combative parent. Put the needs of your children first.

One of the things this book hasn't mentioned is what happens if your children choose to live with your ex-partner and not see you at all (something that is very common in this day and age). This is another huge loss to deal with, on top of the loss of your partner. And if you (like me) are in this situation, please turn to the **Useful resources** at the back of the book where I have listed the best websites (for mothers *or* fathers) and books that I have come across that provide positive ways to help you.

Learning how to cope with this new reality – and even manage your time, as you will have less or more, depending on your absent partner's previous contribution to the house, to the family, to life – is a huge challenge. It helps if you set yourself small daily goals, because then you get the benefit of achieving them.

And when you come across things you can't do – attend parents' evening at school without a babysitter, find a screwdriver to fix the fused plug, pick up a sick child when you are meant to be at work, cook Christmas lunch when your partner always did it, play football or frisbee when all you want is some peace and quiet – then find some help.

✔ It's OK...

... to ask for help.
Use your friends, family, and neighbours, because no one can do everything on their own.

Self-help

Coming to terms with chaos
This exercise is designed to help you cope with change and the resulting chaos, and turn it into... well, something that makes you *think* you are in charge.

So here are three self-help suggestions designed to cope with finances, choices, and tasks – all things that seem impossible, difficult, or end up on lists during divorce (lists that never get done, mind you, thereby adding to the chaos).

1. Deal with finances
There are always massive financial changes with divorce and this is when an Excel spreadsheet is a lifesaver. Knowing exactly what you have to spend (incoming funds) and what you *have* to spend (outgoing funds) takes the fear out of finances. It also lets you take charge of your budget. And it often helps you make decisions about how to fill any shortfall (cutting back? increasing your existing salary? a part-time job or evening babysitting? baking or cooking, or some other skill you have?). So set one up, and update it as bills come in and circumstances change.

2. Deal with choices

There are almost too many choices during divorce because the parameters and boundaries of life as it was have vanished with the marriage. And when you have too many choices or options (do I move abroad? do I move nearer family? do I move nearer their schools?), making any decision is difficult. But you have to pick yourself up and get on with it. The simplest way to organize thoughts is to write them down. So write the decision or dilemma that needs to be sorted at the top of a piece of paper, divide the page into two columns and head one "Pros" and the other "Cons". Then list all things that seem good or bad in the relevant columns, and look at them subjectively. This will allow you to make better choices and weigh them up unemotionally.

3. Deal with chaos

Divorce involves an awful lot of extra work and there is a stage of confronting endless things that need to be done. And when they don't get done, they add to the stress of everyday life. The list is endless – from opening a new bank account, putting the utilities in your name, to changing your will, your passport, medical or holiday insurance, and so on. The trick is to prioritize and accept that everything will get done eventually. So, every week, head a clean piece of paper with "My Try-to-do List" – so named because you might not always succeed in doing everything on the list, but you tried! At the end of each week, look at how many things you *have* done and feel very pleased with yourself, then copy any outstanding things on to next week's list (which makes you try harder and takes the pressure off simultaneously).

6

Starting over
(... the fear factor)

You are now at the stage where you are divorced (the decree absolute is yours, or on its way), the finances are sorted (you have a settlement and a budget), and you have possibly moved house – and everyone thinks the drama is over. Everyone has these huge expectations that you are now starting your "new life". Forgive them, for they probably don't know how scary it still feels inside – overwhelming, looking up a hill, insurmountable. So, with the expectation of others thrown into the pot, you **worry** about everything, and the more you worry, the worse it gets.

My worries at this stage are legendary: *I can't find anything; I won't ever earn enough; I can't face Christmas alone; I can't revive my career as a journalist; I can't retrain; I can't decide what to retrain as; I can't go out; I can't do up that dress; I won't get a mortgage; I can't afford the rent;*

*I can't stop frowning; I can't cope if my children don't speak
to me soon; I won't be able to save for my old age; I will forget
how to laugh; I will die, and several months later someone will
find a wizened old lady with a beard (can't afford electrolysis!)
and no teeth (can't afford the dentist!).* Get the picture?
On bad days, I even worried about why I couldn't stop
worrying!

✔ It's OK...

... to worry.
But be warned: the more you worry, the more worried
you become.

There are several ways to help break the pattern of turning
into a worrywart, but the best way is to look at the root
causes. The only way to stop those niggling thoughts is to
face the fears behind them. And the main fear at this point
is that divorce mucks up all those carefully laid plans for
a happy-ever-after life, and you are meant to create a new
bright world to replace it. *And* create it all alone, and in
double-quick time. Well, God created the world in six
days, with the seventh as a day of rest, but we don't have
those powers, and so the first way of removing that worst
of all fears is to accept it is going to take rather a long
time. But it will happen.

The second underlying fear is a feeling of being cast
adrift. An awful lot of worries stem from unravelling all
the ties that once bound you – family, friends, finances,
home, love, memories, dreams. The important thing is not
to dump all the painful things from your old life because,
believe it or not, you might love them in the future – and

that includes photographs, mementoes, wedding rings, and even people. These things ultimately help anchor you and make you feel safe as you create the new reality.

The third source of fear is that you aren't up to the job. You need to look that one right in the eye – your relationship might have ended with insults and put-downs, but remember that they loved *everything* about you in the beginning. Find your confidence and never give up, be brave and big-hearted, believe in yourself, value your strengths, and rise to the new challenges. And at those inevitable points of meltdown, when you feel you can't cope, remind yourself you already are coping.

 Remember: if you threw your problems in a pile and saw everyone else's, you'd grab yours back.

The fourth fear deep inside is the feeling of being all alone. And you *can* actually be alone because suddenly you are sharing the children, and you have nights or even weeks when they go to visit the other parent. And, before long, you might find you are quite isolated from your old social life, too.

At first the invites flood in, but once the drama is over and the gossip is old news, the stigma of not being "a couple" and being the odd number at the dinner table surfaces. Then some friends who used to be jointly "yours" choose to be solely your ex-partner's – this is hard to accept, but it's not easy for friends either; some can and some can't deal with seeing you both separately.

Even relatives may choose between you. And there are even the "dump you for no reason" friends (who possibly think divorce is contagious!). And the friends who start flirting with you – part of the stigma of divorce is that you are available and looking for fun (which is often the last thing on the divorcee agenda). Plus the friends who try to act as Cupid and match-make. And the friends who invite you to a party – you go alone, have a lovely time, go home, and burst into tears (there's no one there to chat to about it). It is all very complicated, and it takes time and effort to build a new social life (see Chapter 10 for suggestions).

Mythbuster

A divorcee is seen as a threat (or failure) by those who aren't also single.
Not necessarily. But other husbands or wives might need reassuring, and other spouses might need reminding how lucky they are to be married.

The fifth fear is that all these fears won't go away. But they do, and you get used to your new circumstances and eventually embrace them (*I don't have to shop and cook for the children this weekend; I can wear my old floppy running pants and slippers; I can do flat-pack furniture because those bunk beds look great; I might do a dinner party next Saturday*). And in the midst of your worries, remember you do not have to fend for yourself: when times are tough, you find out who your *true* friends are – and these are the ones you must cherish always. Being supported by an immensely kind and loving group of friends and family is the best way to ease your worries, solve your problems, and help you cope.

Coming to terms with worry

Worry is the mind's way of helping you solve problems, so it is important to do that rather than let worrying thoughts niggle away, magnify from molehills to mountains, and take over your life. If you don't address worrying, it makes you tense and edgy, and it can even stop you sleeping or eating. Remember: the thought of the monster under your bed disappears as soon as you look under your bed and see an old sock and a pile of dust!

This little exercise is an effective and efficient way to stop irrational monsters frightening you. It is also a way to let you worry *positively*. There are two parts to the exercise and you need to do it regularly, so set a deadline of, say, a week for the list part, and about twenty minutes once a week for the time part. Gradually, over several weeks, it will enable you to face worries when you choose to, rather than let them dominate your thoughts.

How to tame a worry monster

The Worry List

This is a way of nipping niggles in the bud and postponing nagging thoughts until you can deal with them. It makes you aware of worries and stops them dominating the present. Every time you catch yourself agonizing over something, write it down on a sheet of paper (head it "The Worry List" and keep it handy) and then forget about it, knowing you will worry about it later. It does not matter how many times you write down the same worry, how big or small it is; just list what the worry *actually* is, and nothing else. Then consciously stop thinking about it.

The Worrying Time

This is when you get to look at your worries, for a *maximum* of thirty minutes. Do it at the same time, on the same day, once a week. In response to all listed worries, ask the following questions:

- How likely is it to happen? Is it a real or imagined fear? (This puts things in perspective.)

- If it happened, what would I do? How would I deal with it? (This helps find solutions.)

- How would I advise a friend who had this worry? (This lets you look at it rationally.)

At the end of your allotted time period, switch off and relax. You have done your worrying and if other worries subsequently spring to mind, write them on the next week's Worry List.

7

Think for better
(... forget for worse)

Now it is time to get a grip. No more worrying, wallowing, weeping, woes, wobbles, whatever. OK, they are occasionally acceptable (you are human, after all), but life is passing by and there are adventures to be had, so you need a quick change from desperate divorcee to daredevil divorcee. And the only way you will ever enjoy a brave new world is if you embrace it. That means don't look back, look ahead. Ignore what was lost and find what's to be gained. And, most of all, think **positive**, and forget the negative.

A brave new start needs a new commitment vow – possibly something like: *I imagine a future for better, for richer, in health and happiness, to love and to cherish, to have and to hold, from this day forth.* So make that vow (or make up one of your own), write it on a piece of paper, stick it on your mirror, and recite it every morning as you brush your hair! This will help you on good days (when you spring out of bed) and bad days (when you want to lie there and duvet it).

 Remember: the best *is* yet to come.

But before you can move on positively you need to have made peace with three things from the recent past: they are blame, anger, and change. Although these points might have been sweetly and gently mentioned already, now we have to take a quick, hard look at them (and ourselves!) before it is possible to go any further in the journey of divorce. Properly coming to terms with them is the only way to make that jump and embrace a new life.

Accept some blame
You need to look at your share of the blame for your relationship breakdown and take responsibility for it. One person is never totally responsible, although when emotions are running high, it is normal to blame the other person totally. It is not easy, but try to write down *honestly* your part in the failure of the relationship – it could be "I didn't talk about it", "I didn't notice", or even something about your nature or personality. Try not to be too harsh. This self-analysis will help you move on healthily from your ex-partner, perhaps help you understand how to have better future relationships, and definitely let you live a happier future.

Lose some anger
Even if the outright fury has gone and the burning anger is sporadic, there is still bound to be some resentment

simmering in the most forgiving of human hearts. Resentment is fine, as are flashes of crossness. And real anger is perfectly normal when you first lose something (and you lost your partner, not your left sock!). But with time, burning anger needs to be quenched. So you need to think very carefully about what you really are angry about and let go of it (more about this in the next chapter). Unresolved anger ties you to your ex like a twisting, turning python – and it can squeeze the life out of you.

Be excited by change

The changes that come with divorce are rarely *choices*, so it is very easy to see them as negatives and resent them. They are thrust on you and you have to deal with them. So, before you can start to be positive about the new life, you have to accept that change is inevitable (it would be happening even if you were still married), and it is how you *choose* to deal with it that matters. Accepting this frees you from anger and blame and lets you envisage a more exciting life ahead.

Coming to terms with these three things will be your salvation. In life, the only way to forget and move on is to forgive.

Mythbuster

Nobody ever totally gets over the pain of divorce. Not true. Because despite the fact that divorce is never an amicable thing, life is too precious to waste it hating anyone or looking back at what might have been.

How to think positive

The next way to help jump from the old life (past) to the new (future) is to shrug off the "victim" response. When you are at the receiving end of hurt, pain, and what feels like punishment, it is very easy to take it and accept it and even think you will never be happy (so you must deserve all this negativity). This is the victim response. And then it becomes easier to look for the worst in situations (to be prepared for disappointment) than to find the best (and risk disappointment).

The way to break the habit is to be aware every time you see something as a minus, a problem, or a negative, and make a *conscious and deliberate* decision to turn it into a plus, a bonus, or a positive. I call this the "Pollyanna" response (and if you ever saw the 1960 Walt Disney film starring Hayley Mills, you will know why!), which is quite simply looking for the best in every situation. And it is a lifesaver.

A few examples:

- Turn "I never thought our relationship would end" into "I did everything in my power to save our relationship".

- Turn "I so regret wasting twenty years of my life in that relationship" into "At one time it was what I wanted".

- My all-time favourite, from the actress Lana Turner: turn "I planned on having one husband and seven children" into "It turned out the other way around"!

- My current favourite: turn "I will never finish this book by the deadline" into "Oh, I am already up to Chapter 7"!

Try it – it really does work.

How to act positive

Positive thoughts can be turned into positive actions, which is vital in everyday life. After all, to live a life we must *do* twice as much as we *think*. The most obvious example occurring about now in the divorce journey is that you have to downsize – half the space, half the possessions, half the assets. This definitely requires positive action: I chose to sell everything I did not like, need, or want on the internet (a friend taught me how, with a crash course on the intricacies of the ebay website), and then use the funds to start creating my own new space (the ex liked antiques, I like modern furniture; the ex liked venetian blinds, I like daylight).

Starting again, choosing what you want, and making it happen – in all areas of life – is what's exciting about letting go of the past and creating a new future. So, to embrace a new life, approach it as positive, and then take positive steps to make it happen.

A few examples:

- Turn "This new home is so small and dark" into "I am going to paint the walls white and clean the windows".

- Turn "I can't leave work, do a shop, and pick up the kids in time" into "Let's have a takeaway tonight".

- My all-time *imaginary* favourite: turn "I can knit" into "I am a famous multimillionaire artist who creates coats for small dogs and hamsters".

- My current favourite: turn "This book is taking up my every waking moment" into "Next month I will have the time to relax, go to bed early, and stay in bed late".

Try it – it really does work.

... to think your current life is unsatisfactory.
But only you can turn it into the life *you* want.

Coming to terms with tomorrow
This might be the best self-help exercise so far. You get to exorcize the demons, bury the past, and see into the future. Not many speedy, simple, fun, and free self-help exercises can deliver that! So this is what you have to do next: focus on all that you did not like about your old life. This could range from always leaving clothes lying on the floor to verbal abuse in front of the children. Then focus on all that you like about your new life. This could range from more free time to being free to make your own decisions.

But along the way of letting it all out, think positive and think about your future dreams, plans, and adventures (no matter how impossible). And in this exercise you can be as negative as you want for one last time (just let rip and write down every little detail), because you get to be positive, too. After all, the basis of accountancy is that pluses and minuses cancel each other out.

You need a sheet of paper and a pen. Symbolically, draw a line down the middle of the page and one across, near the top. Then at the top of the columns write "All the negatives of my old life" in one, and "All the positives of my new life" in the other. Then list them.

Once you have done it, you *will* feel better and more positive. And studies show that positive people are happier and more successful at anything and everything they tackle in life.

8

Vengeance is mine (... said the divorcee)

This is where we get to talk about all the things we are not meant to feel, let alone mention – vengeance, retribution, **revenge**, spite, anger, getting even, venom, grudges, just deserts, wrath, hatred, tit for tat, an eye for an eye, comeuppance. Now we have got the nastiness out in the open – and bearing in mind we are meant to be moving on in our journey – how do we deal with it?

It's a cliché, but it's true that the best revenge is having a happy, successful life because, trust me, no ex-partner wants to see you forgetting them, getting over them, and living quite happily without them. They might pretend they don't care, but deep down they feel as rejected inside as you – even if they chose to end the relationship.

All feelings of wanting revenge spring from a sense of being badly treated, which in turn creates a dark, seething fury very different from pure anger. Not being able to right a sense of injustice, unfairness, rejection, humiliation, and wrongs leads to feeling thwarted or hard done by – and that is what feeds the vengeful soul. But, quite frankly, life is unfair sometimes, and feeling bitter about what life has dealt you contaminates everything else, and that includes your current enjoyment, your future hopes, your friendships, your children's lives, and possibly even your grandchildren's.

So your ultimate choice in this chapter is between "Why *should* I let my ex get away with it?" and "Why should I let it go?"

Don't get mad

It is important at this stage in the new life to rely on your own strengths – and this includes morals and personal integrity. It is a good time to try to be the bigger person, to be gracious and hold on to whatever dignity you can muster. No matter how excruciatingly painful it is, now is the time to smile, grit your teeth, and only make positive or neutral comments about your ex-partner in public. A deadly divorcee is not a pretty sight (and it stops you moving on from the desperate to daredevil stage). Since life is about moving on, be warned that, with time, even the most patient and kind people will avoid a desperate divorcee like the plague.

So, in private, to a close, trusted friend, say whatever you are really thinking (and let go of it), and apart from that bite your tongue.

✔ It's OK...

... to speak your mind.
But *think* before you speak because once you have said
something it can never be taken back.

Don't get even

You know your ex-partner better than anyone; you know
their funny little ways and weaknesses, and you probably
know how to get even. But...

- *Don't* reveal the secrets of their tax returns to the
  taxman.

- *Don't* tell their life insurance company about those little
  white lies.

- *Don't* lace their cup of tea with laxative.

- *Don't* push fresh prawns through their letterbox when
  they go on holiday.

- *Don't* make a life-size effigy of them, dress it in their
  Gucci boots, and chuck it on a bonfire.

The reason I say *don't* is because it doesn't make you
feel better for long. And I should know, because I did
one of the five don'ts listed above! Just confessing that
makes me feel better, but I am still too ashamed to admit
which one it was, so you'll just have to guess (go to www.
pennyrichthewriter.com to see if you guessed right!). If it
makes you feel better, *do* have an "Out with the old" party
("divorce" parties don't sound right somehow) and make
the entertainment a re-edit of your wedding video (so you
take back the kiss, take back the ring, leave the church,

and drive off!). This way, at least you are acknowledging the frustration within (and letting go of it) but you will still be able to sleep at night with a clear conscience.

Mythbuster

Revenge makes you feel better.
No, it doesn't! Doing unto others as you would be done by makes everyone feel better (but feel free to imagine doing whatever you wish).

There is one last thing to consider if you want the best revenge (remember? No, it's *not* spreading wicked rumours about your ex-partner! It is a happy, successful life), and that is, how can you let go of all that resentment? Easy, if you look at how much divorce has changed *you*, because on some levels your ex-partner must have changed, too. And you have both (we hope) accepted some blame, so you should understand that we are not perfect, we all have flaws, and we are all fallible. But the real reason to let it all go is forgiveness. Once you forgive, you can forget and move on.

 Remember: (almost) everyone deserves a second chance.

Self-help

Coming to terms with forgiveness
This exercise is designed to help you finally let go of bad feelings and feel good. In a word: forgiveness. It is not a fashionable word, but it is a very, very important one when it comes to revenge. So you are going to try, finally,

once and for all, to let go of all that past stuff and look ahead. What you are going to do is look at why you are pleased your ex-partner is not part of your future life – but in an imaginary way, which is what the best revenge should be.

The last self-help exercise looked at the negative and plus points; this one looks at the things they did to you (real or imagined) that you dislike, then lists the revenge (imagined) that would bring atonement.

So you need another sheet of clean paper and a pen. Draw another symbolic line down the middle of the page and one across, near the top. Then, at the top of the two columns, write "The things they did (real or imagined) that I hate" in one, and "The things (imagined) I would like to do to feel better" in the other. Next, fill the columns in, writing whatever you wish. Finally, you are going to set fire to the evidence, because no one should read it but you (in therapy terms, the burning is a physical letting go). And, after that, everything is much closer to being forgiven and forgotten. Forgiveness brings peace of mind.

P.S. You are allowed one thing you *never* forgive your ex for. Choose it wisely!

9

The ex factor (... how to win that game)

By now, if this book has been any use at all, you should be able to accept that not everything about your ex-partner is bad. The thing is, of course, your ex-partner might not have read this book! So you might still be on the receiving end of blame, accusations, and poor communication. There will be loose ends you need to discuss, and if you have children, ongoing plans or decisions that need both parents' input. Learning how to **communicate** positively is vital from here on.

After a relationship has broken down irreconcilably, some people stay friends very easily while others prefer to be enemies. Bear in mind it is *your* relationship that is broken; do *not* let it break up the family – so it is very important to put children's needs first here. Also, bear in mind that being friendly (for the sake of all parties concerned) is very different from being friends. No one expects you to share a slow candlelit dinner, quick latte, short shower, or long holiday any more – unless you feel completely at ease doing so. But even sworn to-the-death enemies, such as cowboys and Indians, could raise a white flag to enable peace talks.

What often stops peaceful talks in present times is something I will politely call white noise – or the many background voices that add to any ongoing discussions, particularly if your ex already has a new partner. New partners, in the first flush of it all, are listened to, and so their needs, opinions, and wishes do influence decisions, whether you like it or not. And if you have a new partner, some of their opinions (as they try to help you) will also get thrown into the pot.

The other cause of communication breakdown is what I will (again) politely call past disagreement. There are many ways of talking, and in long-term relationships any discussions, negotiations, and interactions become predictable – we play the same roles and have the same conversations, again and again. So you are probably still communicating the way you did in your relationship – not really listening to each other, reacting defensively, and even repeating the same entrenched views. Some of the roles we slip into are:

- *The blackmailer*: "If you give me that, I'll do this..."

- *The boss*: "You should do (not do) that..."

- *The baby*: "Oh, please. I'll be good and come home at x time... only spend x amount..."

- *The bickerer*: "I don't want to... Why should I...? Don't tell me what to do..."

- *The superior*: "Don't be silly/stupid/mad... You don't know what you're talking about..."
- *The inferior*: "You're right, it's just that... I know I don't understand, but..."

Recognize any of those from the past? We all do, but our relationship with the ex-partner (and the way we dealt with it once) is over. Now we need to communicate in a new, adult way – which is how we communicate with our colleagues at work (*I need that report at the end of the week, please*), figures of authority such as headteachers, doctors, or bank managers (*I want to know if I can...*), and our friends (*Be great to catch up. When is it OK for you?*). We take the emotion out of adult conversation for a very good reason – it means we are more likely to get the result we want.

 Remember: even if you dislike your ex-partner, be polite – there are some days you hate your boss and you don't let on!

So, now that we understand the rules, let's look at the best possible way of communicating with the ex-partner from now on.

The rules of ex-communication

Down to business: forget the old boardroom (or bedroom) agenda, ignore new white noise, and look to the future – the "whiteboard" approach, which is wiping the page clean and starting again. From now on, you are only an adult speaking to another adult, to try to sort stuff out – which means you have to relearn how to speak and how to listen. If you follow the rules below, you are more likely to get the solution you are aiming for from your ex-partner. As any politician knows, how you pitch it, how you deflect unwanted interruptions, and how reasonable you appear to be all determine your personal success or failure.

Mythbuster

Relationships end with disagreements that leave both partners angry and bitter.
Yes, this one is true! But that was in the past, and the way you *both* choose to act in the here and now will determine the future.

Here is the beginner's guide to grown-up communication. And it does not matter whether it's by email, text, or phone – this will help you steer the dialogue, and respond to it, to get results. These are the rules for communicating with your ex-partner from now on:

Be prepared
Think of a business meeting! Be businesslike and plan what you need to say beforehand. Think in statements, so no "I thinks", "you shoulds", or "you musts". Also, look at how they might respond, and how you will handle their response. You need to decide if you are requesting something (negotiable), asking for something (non-negotiable), or suggesting something (with options).

Be considerate
Think manners! Arrange a time to have the conversation, if it is verbal, so it suits both of you. You don't want to

be tired or distracted, and you don't want to phone your partner when they are at a party. This is forward planning, in the best sense, since good timing equals good tactics.

Be polite
Think of your bank manager! This means no personal comments, no irrelevant outbursts, "no shoulds" or "musts", and no mention at all of past events. And, above all, breathe deeply, keep calm, and do not raise your voice or put emotion into what should be a reasonable discussion. If it is by email, send a reasonable, brief, and necessary pitch.

Be quiet
Think mute! Being cool, calm, and collected and leaving pauses when you don't speak gives you time to think. It also makes your partner feel you are listening to, and considering, their comments (which you *must* do). It also stops you babbling nervously and saying something you might regret.

Be patient
Think of the goal! If they don't "hear" your message, repeat it calmly. Say you understand their point of view, but ask if there is any compromise you could reach (options, negotiation). Keep repeating only that you think it would be good to reach a mutual decision on this one in response to anything angry, vitriolic, or personal that they say.

Be in charge
Think of the bigger picture! If the conversation does not give the results you hoped for, end it positively. Don't

try to argue them into agreeing, because it won't work. Instead, suggest that you both think about it and talk again. And before you hang up or leave, try to arrange a time when you can do that.

... to agree to disagree.
You don't have to win every argument.

Sometimes, in some relationships, the end really is the end. If your ex-partner chooses not to communicate with you, there is nothing much more you can do apart from accept it – and I can say this honestly, since mine decided not to see or contact me more than a year ago. But do not use your children as go-betweens to deliver requests or messages – it just makes them feel a division of loyalty or that they are taking sides. And do, when you feel strong enough, keep trying: time is a great healer, so (fingers crossed!) eventually you might manage to communicate with your ex-partner in a positive way.

OK, one last thing to discuss about dealing with the ex-partner – it's time to add an "S" to "ex"...

Sex without the ex
The first difficult thing to discuss is how you deal with meeting the person who is now having sex (you presume) with your ex-partner. Until you feel ready to do so, try to avoid it. If an act of God means you accidently run into them outside a teashop in Cornwall, be as charming and pleasant as you can and move on. If you are big enough to accept the new partner, do it on your own terms –

so set clear boundaries for possible mutual meeting events (school plays, weddings, graduations, family parties, and so on) to avoid uncomfortable surprises or embarrassment. If your boundaries are ignored and you then issue "either/or" ultimatums, bear in mind that you will have to accept other people's choices – made by friends, family, even your own children – and they may not choose *you*. The hard fact is, in modern times there are so many intertwined relationships (stepchildren, stepmothers, half brothers and sisters, two fathers in one family, granny-in-laws) that you must either learn to accept all of them in an open-hearted way or ban them from your life.

The first rule if *you* have a new partner is to try to resist showing off! Apart from that, if you have lost one important relationship in your life, you are old enough to make your own decisions. Some people already have the new partner (even before the end of the marriage, let alone the separation or divorce). Others replace their ex very quickly after the decree absolute. Other people need time before they can even contemplate finding someone else. And then there are those who are quite happy never to have a relationship again. No right or wrong here, just a brief, polite, and possibly unnecessary conversation about S.E.X.

Self-help

Coming to terms with yapping

This self-help exercise is a long-term project. Think of it as behavioural training – the sort of thing happily married couples have to do with new puppies. Bearing in mind that the second definition of "yap" in the *Oxford English Dictionary* (Oxford University Press) is "to talk at length in an irritating manner", this exercise is designed purely to help deal with phone conversations, texts, or emails that come with blame and accusations.

Eventually, with time, the person at the other end of the phone or keyboard will learn what they have to do to get the response they want, or, indeed, any response at all, much as dogs do. This will save you much stress and therefore guarantee you are happier and live longer than the yapper!

Barking up the wrong tree...
When you are on the receiving end of long and involved phone calls from your ex-partner, you can eventually retrain them:

- Be polite at first, even if the number flashed up and you know who the caller is.

- Then, if there is much you do not wish to hear, *go deaf*: imagine you are somewhere else, or you are a rock and it is all water washing over you (or any other imagery that works).

- Occasionally, say something non-committal but audible (*Hmmmm... OK... ahah... ohhhh*), but leave very long pauses between murmurs, and still don't say *anything* else.

- Eventually even the most dogged person will run out of steam and possibly get to the poin. If they do, reply to the point, cheerfully and politely (the reward). If they run out of steam and stop yapping *without* getting to a point, say it was nice talking to them and hang up (the hint of a reward).

If you receive calls that are actually menacing or threatening, or persistent, speak to the police and your telephone service provider about what you should do. If you don't play ball, eventually they will realize they are barking up the wrong tree and will find another one to bark at. They will also learn that if they behave nicely, they might get what they want.

Yap email

When you are on the receiving end of long, sometimes vitriolic but always involved emails from your ex-partner, you can eventually retrain them:

- First, open the email, read it, and press "Forward". Then type your ex's email address in the "To" box.

- Next, move the cursor to their original message and highlight in yellow (it is sunny and bright!) any important *facts* or *points* they raise that you wish to reply to. If there are none, ignore this step and, after reading the email, don't press "Forward", just press "Delete" instead.

- Start your message with "Dear (*name*)" and simply reply to the *facts* or *points* you have highlighted in their original, forwarded message. Add nothing else, and nothing personal or emotive. Then press "Send".

If you continue to play dead, eventually they will roll over! Or at least they will realize they can't yank your lead.

10

To love and to cherish (... from this day forth)

Now it is time to take off the hair shirt, shed the sack cloth and ashes, believe in miracles, and **rejoice** in the possibilities that lie ahead – well, that's what happens in the last chapter of fairy stories, but (sigh) this is real life. You might not be ready yet, you might already be rejoicing, but trust me, at some point in the future you will look back on divorce as just another chapter in life.

 Remember: no one is in charge of your future happiness but you.

Before we consider ways of enjoying a better future, let's do a final stocktake of the present: first, look at how far you have come, what you have survived, and all that you have coped with since your relationship ended. You should feel proud of yourself. No one is suggesting that you have reached happy-ever-after, or even the middle of the divorce journey yet, and that there won't be struggles and tough times ahead. But just by reading the previous chapters you have come a long way – and learned a few tricks, techniques, and practical tips to help deal with whatever is happening now and whatever lies ahead.

You will have realized you are not alone; that the turmoil and everything else you are feeling is perfectly normal and to be expected; that there is no right or wrong in dealing with loss, and everybody should deal with it in their own way, at their own pace.

You will have learned a few things about yourself that even you didn't know before; that you are neither Prince Charming nor Snow White, because human beings are not perfect – we all have faults, foibles, and flaws that we have to understand, accept, and live with. And, most important, I hope you have learned to love and cherish yourself, see your strengths, and be kind to and forgiving of whatever burdens lie in your heart.

My own divorce was finalized in 2009, and I am happy to admit I am still not "over it". But I am busy enjoying a positive future, which is what all divorcees must try to aim for and rejoice in achieving. Here are some of the things that are vital to help you do just that.

A friend in deed

The best advice for a happy future is to surround yourself with good friends who make you laugh and support and love you, no matter what. They are the ones who will babysit, hold your hand, hold a ladder, pin the trouser hem, be there in an emergency – all the things you can't do alone. One of the great lessons of divorce is how wonderful *true* friends are. Those who have chosen you made that choice for a reason. So be a very good friend back, from now on and for always, and do anything and everything for them, particularly if they are in trouble – and even at a time when you might have insurmountable problems of your own.

Also, it is important to listen to friendly advice – you might not agree with it, but friends often suggest things that really are in your best interest, even if it might not feel like it then and there. Friends are great motivators, so keep an open mind.

The lone star

The best way to deal with loneliness is to embrace it. If you haven't got a partner now, you might feel alone or even lonely at times, but you can rise above it and see the positive *if* you choose to. Since you first married, there probably hasn't been a time when you haven't chosen to accommodate a partner's needs or compromise your own dreams. Now you can do whatever you choose, whatever you want to do, as you only have yourself to please.

Which means this is the first time in your adult life that it is OK to be selfish! You need to recognize that and enjoy it, because you may choose to put a future partner's needs before your own sooner than you imagine.

Mythbuster

It is lonely being a divorcee.
No! Two people in an unhappy marriage can feel lonelier than a happy person alone.

Now is a good time to look back on all the things you wanted to do but didn't, and fill your empty moments with achieving those dreams. Do not sit at home alone, moping. Here are some thoughts to inspire you:

- Release the creative side: learn a language, a musical instrument, how to draw, paint, make pots, mosaics, how to sew, write, or decorate cakes.

- Release the physical side: get fit and exercise (running, walking, swimming, a DVD), take up a sport (rowing, tennis, flying, sailing), take up a relaxing, de-stressing class (massage, stretch, meditation).

- Release the mind: learn a new skill (computers, counselling, beautician, alternative therapies, how to run a business).

- Release the adventurer: go to art galleries, the theatre, a foreign country, volunteer to help your community, volunteer for a charity, learn to tango or salsa.

Remind yourself that you can't do any of these things – and you certainly won't make new friends or meet anyone – if you sit at home.

Lonely hearts

The best romantic advice for a divorcee is to be realistic about about the chances of finding someone else. Your friends may start to say it is time to "move on", "take the plunge", and put yourself "out there". This is because they think you are wonderful and deserve to have someone who appreciates and loves you. So let's be realistic about your options:

- The last time you dated was probably pre-internet. And internet dating is a modern minefield. If you are considering it, be aware that you will have to take on (more) rejection before you possibly meet "the one".

- Love is only lovelier the second time around if you have learned from your previous experience – and, if so, you probably have a gorgeous new partner already. If not, be aware that you could be going from "out of the frying pan" into "the fire", so use your head as well as your heart as you consider new love.

- If you never get the chance to meet someone, don't fret about it. Fate throws things your way when you least expect it. And in the meantime, if you are positive, happy, joyful, and enthusiastic about life, it will show – you will glow with it. And since moths always rush to the light, watch out.

From this day forth

The last advice to enable you to embrace whatever comes next is to look forward, not backward. You need to live in the "now" and be positive, rather than looking back at what might have been or ahead to what might be. Living in the now means when the next challenge or disaster comes your way (and life is full of them, even without divorce), you will be better prepared, not panic, and be *positive* and ask yourself, "In five years' time, will this matter?" You might even start to think, "I have gained more than I have lost." Wouldn't that be wonderful?

By achieving this, you will treasure your friends, make the most of the present, and be surprised by what the future brings. If you are able to manage this, you will have a rich and rewarding life – more adventurous, successful, creative, outgoing, joyful, and happy than the past one.

Because in life...

... to make mistakes.
We all make them, but the trick is to learn from them. And how you deal with them is what matters most.

Self-help

Coming to terms with joyfulness
The final self-help exercise is designed to let you rejoice in your journey so far. It might have started with you staring into divorce alley (a dead-end street) but it will, when you get there, finish with you as the daredevil divorcee – strong, brave, self-confident, living life to the full, accepting the downs, and enjoying every moment of the ups.

To help you on the way, grab a sheet of paper and a pen, and scrawl across the top, in capital letters, MY REASONS TO BE CHEERFUL LIST. Then start listing all the reasons you can think of – and keep adding to this list as time goes by, as often as you want. One day, it will be the diary of your life.

P.S. If you manage to achieve even half of what you have read in this book, then peace *will* be with you. I hope so.

For the family

Separation and divorce impact on family and friends nearly as much as the couple whose relationship is ending. Here are a few very basic pointers to help you deal with the fallout, but please look on the websites in the **Useful resources** section at the back of the book – most of them offer fantastic advice, contacts, and support for children, extended family, and friends.

For children

- Your parents are divorcing – *you* aren't. So you should feel free to love both of them.

- You do not need to take sides.

- This is not *your fault*.

- Life goes on and in a few years your new home life will seem "normal".

- You can't fix everything, but be loving and kind to your parents even if they act differently for a while (shout, cry, etc.).

- If you don't like the way your parents behave, tell them, or write them a note – it is important they know how you are feeling.

- Almost one in two families split up, so many of your friends have lived through it and you are not alone.

For friends and family

- Be a good listener as they pour out the emotional turmoil inside. And they will call you, day or night, at the most inconvenient times!

- Be sympathetic. You don't have to tell them what to do, just gently help them debate their choices (even if you disagree with what they say they are going to do!).

- Be positive and uplifting. You need to give them hope, love, and praise, and keep reminding them that they can get through this (and the future will be rosy).

- Be supportive. They might need help with money, child care, going to see a counsellor or lawyer. If you can, organize a team of friends/family to share the burden (it will help everyone).

- Be available. If you can arrange some "normal" social life during this abnormal time, it might make everyone else forget their pain, stress, and worries (briefly!). For example, pop around with a takeaway at night or have a family lunch together at the weekend, a trip to the cinema, a long walk, or any other exercise.

 And remember, one day you will *all* look back on this as a distant memory.

Useful resources

United Kingdom

For counselling, mediation, legal

Relate
Relate offers help with relationships for couples, parents,
or families – advice, counselling, mediation, workshops,
and support.
Tel: 0300 100 1234
Website: www.relate.org.uk

National Family Mediation
A network of family mediation services in the UK to help
those affected by separation and divorce.
Tel: 0300 4000 636
Website: www.nfm.org.uk

Samaritans
Confidential 24-hour support for anyone experiencing
despair, distress, or suicidal feelings.
Tel: 08457 90 90 90 UK or 1850 60 90 90 Republic of Ireland
Website: www.samaritans.org

Depression Alliance
Leading UK charity for people affected by depression.
Tel: 0845 123 23 20
Website: www.depressionalliance.org

Legal information

Directgov
A public service site that includes legal information on separation and divorce.
Website: www.directgov.gov.uk

Resolution
Resolution's 6,000 members are family lawyers who adhere to a code of practice promoting a non-confrontational approach to divorce and separation.
Tel: 01689 820272
Website: www.resolution.org.uk

Relationships Scotland
Counselling, mediation, and family support throughout Scotland.
Tel: 0845 119 2020
Website: www.relationships-scotland.org.uk

For children and families

ChildLine
A free, 24-hour helpline offering confidential advice to young people in the UK.
Tel: 0800 1111
Website: www.childline.org.uk

Divorce Aid
A professional and independent website offering advice, support, and information on all aspects of divorce and separation for adults and children, with links to other sites.
Website: www.divorceaid.co.uk

For non-resident parents

MATCH (Mothers Apart from Their Children)
A UK-wide support and self-help group for women living apart from their children.
Website: www.matchmothers.org

FNF (Families Need Fathers)
A UK-wide support group that helps with shared parenting issues after family breakdown.
Tel: 0300 0300 363
Website: www.fnf.org.uk

Australia

For counselling, mediation, legal

Family Relationship Centres
Offers local counselling, support, and legal and practical help for families.
Tel: 1800 050 321
Website: www.familyrelationships.gov.au

Lifeline
Confidential 24-hour support for anyone experiencing despair, distress, or suicidal feelings.
Tel: 13 11 14
Website: www.lifeline.org.au

For children

Kids Helpline
Free 24-hour telephone support for 5- to 25-year-olds.
Tel: 1800 55 1800
Website: www.kidshelp.com.au

For non-resident parents

Lone Fathers Association of Australia
Advice and support for fathers or mothers apart from their children.
Website: www.lonefathers.com.au

Canada

For counselling, mediation, legal

Families Change
Online support for children, teens, and parents during separation or divorce.
Website: www.familieschange.ca

Crisis Line
Confidential 24-hour support for anyone experiencing despair, distress, or suicidal feelings.
Tel: 613 722 6914 (within Ottawa); 1 866 996 0991 (outside Ottawa)
Website: www.crisisline.ca

Divorce in Canada
Government-funded online advice on divorce in Canada.
Website: www.divorceincanada.ca

For children

Kids Help Phone
Free 24-hour telephone support for 5- to 25-year-olds.
Tel: 1 800 668 6868
Website: www.kidshelpphone.ca

For non-resident parents

Fathers are Capable Too
Promotes equal shared parenting for both mothers and fathers.
Website: www.fact.on.ca

New Zealand

For counselling, mediation, legal

Relationship Services
A nationwide relationship counselling service for couples, parents, or families.
Website: www.relate.org.nz

LifeLine
For confidential 24-hour telephone support, advice, and counselling.
Tel: 0800 543 354
Website: www.lifeline.co.nz

New Zealand Government
Government guidelines on separation or divorce in New Zealand.
Website: www.newzealand.govt.nz

For children

Kidsline
Confidential 24-hour free telephone advice for under 14-year-olds.
Tel: 0800 KIDSLINE
Website: www.kidsline.org.nz

For non-resident parents
MENZ
Promotes shared parenting and offers advice and support.
Website: www.menz.org.nz

United States

For counselling, mediation, legal

American Association for Marriage and Family Therapy
For information on therapies and a nationwide accredited therapist locator.
Tel: 703 838 9808
Website: www.aamft.org

Divorce Support
For information on all areas of divorce, including individual state laws.
Website: www.divorcesupport.com

National Suicide Prevention Lifeline
For confidential, 24-hour, free telephone advice, support, and counselling.
Tel: 1 800 273 TALK
Website: www.suicidepreventionlifeline.org

 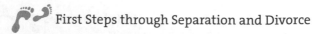

For children

Boys Town National Hotline
Confidential, 24-hour free telephone advice for children.
Tel: 1 800 448 3000
Website: www.boystown.org

Kids Turn
An interactive website for children of divorce seeking advice and support. From the home page follow the link to "Hot Topics", then "Social Issues", then "Children of Divorce".
Website: www.kidsturncentral.com

For non-resident parents

American Coalition for Fathers and Children
Aims to promote shared parenting, and offers advice and support.
Website: www.acfc.org

Useful books

John Bolch, *Do Your Own Divorce: A Practical Guide to Divorcing without a Lawyer*, How To Books, 2009.

Steve Davies, *The Divorced Dad's Handbook: Practical Help and Reassurance for All Fathers Made Absent by Divorce or Separation*, How To Books, 2006.

Paula Hall, *Help Your Children Cope with Your Divorce: A Relate Guide*, Vermilion, 2007.

Paula Hall, *How to Have a Healthy Divorce: A Relate Guide*, Vermilion, 2008.

Sarah Hart, *A Mother Apart: How to Let Go of Guilt and Find Happiness Living Apart from Your Child*, Crown House Publishing, 2008.

Vicki Lansky, *Divorce Book for Parents: Helping Your Children with Divorce and Its Aftermath*, Book Peddlars, 1996.

Richard A. Warshak, *Divorce Poison: How to Protect Your Family from Badmouthing and Brainwashing*, HarperPaperbacks, 2010.

There are also many excellent fictional books for children of all ages on the theme of divorce (at all good bookshops or search on www.amazon.co.uk).

Also currently available in the "First Steps" series:

First Steps out of Anxiety
Dr Kate Middleton

First Steps through Bereavement
Sue Mayfield

First Steps out of Depression
Sue Atkinson

First Steps out of Eating Disorders
Dr Kate Middleton
and Jane Smith

First Steps out of Problem Drinking
John McMahon

First Steps out of Problem Gambling
Lisa Mills and Joanna Hughes

Forthcoming in 2012:

First Steps through the Menopause
Catherine Francis

First Steps out of Weight Problems
Catherine Francis